Improve your aural!

Paul Harris

Contents

FABER ff MUSIC

Why is aural important?

You may wonder why you have to do aural at all. It's because it will help you – perhaps more than *any other* single musical skill – to improve as an all-round musician.

Aural is all about understanding and processing music that you hear and see, *in your head*. By doing so, you will find that your own playing improves enormously. You will be able to play more expressively and stylistically, be more sensitive to quality and control of tone, improve your sight-reading, spot your own mistakes, be more sensitive to others when playing or singing in an ensemble, be more aware of intonation, improve your ability to memorise music and improve your ability to improvise and compose.

All the many elements of musical training are of course connected. So, when working through the activities in this book you will be connecting with many of them. You'll be listening, singing, clapping, playing your instrument, writing music down, improvising and composing – as well as developing that vital ability to do well at the aural tests in your grade exams!

Aural is not an occasional optional extra – just to be taken off a dusty shelf a few days (or even hours) before a music exam. It's something you can be developing and thinking about all the time. And as you go through the enjoyable and fun activities in these books you'll realise how important and useful having a good musical ear or being 'good at aural' really is.

How to use this book

When you have a few minutes to spare (perhaps at the beginning or end of a practice session), sit down with your instrument, by your CD player, and open this book. Choose a section and then work through the activities – you needn't do much each time. But whatever you do, do it carefully, repeating any activity if you feel it will help. In fact many of the activities will be fun to do again and again. And make sure that you come back to the book on a regular basis.

The answers to all the questions in this book are available to download in PDF format from fabermusic.com

So, good luck and enjoy improving your aural skills!

Paul Harris

> **For U.S. readers:**
> Bar = Measure
> Note = Tone
> Tone = Whole step
> Semitone = Half step

Grade 7

Pitch

Singing (or playing) the lower part of a two-part phrase

This is really no more difficult than singing the *upper* part of a two-part phrase! But you do need to concentrate your listening carefully.

Listening activities

CD1 track 2 | **1** In this first set of examples you will hear a short three-note phrase in two parts. Each part is played by a different instrument. After you've heard each example, sing the lower part. Use your pause control between examples if you need more time.

CD1 track 3 | **2** In the next six examples the two parts are again played by contrasting instruments – after you've heard each one twice, sing the lower part. The lower line will then be played for you to check.

CD1 track 4 | **3** You will hear the six examples again, just once this time. Write down on which degree of the scale the lower part ends.

1 _____   2 _____   3 _____

4 _____   5 _____   6 _____

CD1 track 5 | **4** The next set of examples is played on the piano – as in the exam. Listen carefully to each one and then sing the lower part. Again the lower line will then be repeated for you to check your answer.

CD1 track 6 | **5** In Grade 8 you have to sing back the lowest of three parts. Here's some early practice for you! You'll hear the examples on two different instruments (the upper two lines will be played by the same instrument) which will help you to hear the lowest part more easily. Sing after you've heard the phrase twice.

Sight-singing from notation

In Grade 7 you will have to sight-sing a four-bar phrase with single line piano accompaniment.

Listening activities

1 Hear each of the following phrases in your head. Look carefully for scale and arpeggio patterns and how the music relates to the keynote. Then listen to them being played on the track. Each will have two melodic changes. Circle the notes that have been altered.

2 Now sing each phrase *as is written*. You will be given the key chord for each example. After a pause you will hear the phrase for you to check your answer.

3 All the following examples have a bass line added. Study each example, hearing it as best you can in your head first. Look for scale and arpeggio patterns and see how the upper line relates to the lower line, both rhythmically and melodically. Then play the track, pausing between each example.

Cadences

The *interrupted cadence* is introduced at Grade 7. Using the punctuation analogy, this cadence is perhaps best represented by a question mark. Its effect is to delay the end of a phrase. Like a perfect cadence, an interrupted cadence begins with chord V but is then followed by chord VI (rather than chord I).

V   VI

There is an element of surprise about an interrupted cadence! Listen to the example on this track.

1 On this track you'll hear four interrupted cadences in baroque, classical, romantic and 20th/21st-century style. Connect the boxes.

Baroque style	played 1st
Classical style	played 2nd
Romantic style	played 3rd
20th/21st-Century style	played 4th

2 Here are nine cadences. They will be perfect (V – I), imperfect (I/IV – V) or interrupted (V – VI). Describe the cadence and then write down the two chords. The first one is done for you.

1   *Imperfect I – V*   2 _____

3 _____   4 _____

5 _____   6 _____

7 _____   8 _____

9 _____

3 Here are some more examples. Write down the cadence, chords and whether the phrase was in a major or minor key.

1 _____

2 _____

3 _____

4 _____

5 _____

6 _____

Modulations

Pieces of music are rarely written without moving through different keys. The process of moving from one key to another is called *modulation*. This adds variety, colour and tension to a work.

Listening activities 1

1 In each of this first set of examples you will hear a musical phrase made up of five chords. Write down whether the final chord is the same as the first chord (S) in which case there has been no modulation, or if it's a different chord (M) indicating a modulation has taken place.

1 _____   2 _____   3 _____   4 _____   5 _____

2 In the next, longer examples listen carefully and decide whether the piece ends in the same key (S) or has modulated to a new key (M).

1 _____   2 _____   3 _____   4 _____   5 _____

In Grade 7 there are three possible keys for music to modulate to. They are:
- The *sub-dominant* key (e.g. if we begin in C major, then a modulation to F major)
- The *dominant* key (e.g. if we begin in C major, then a modulation to G major)
- The *relative minor* key (e.g. if we begin in C major, then a modulation to A minor)

Modulating to the relative minor (i.e. a modulation from a major key to a minor key) is easy to spot. The other two need more practice. Some try to remember the keynote of the opening key (often by singing it quietly while the music is being played) and then relating it to the new keynote at the end of the example. This may work, but is not recommended – it can be unreliable.

A modulation to the dominant key (V) requires the sharpening of the 4th degree of the scale, producing a brightening effect. Listen to track 16.

A modulation to the sub-dominant key (IV) requires a lowering of the 7th degree of the scale, producing a flattening effect. Listen to track 17.

As you listen to more examples you will become more and more confident in hearing the moment when the key changes.

Listening activities 2

3 In this set of exercises, modulations will only be to the sub-dominant (IV) or dominant (V). Listen for the flattening of the 7th (IV) or the sharpening of the 4th (V). Write down IV or V.

1 _____   2 _____   3 _____   4 _____   5 _____

6 _____   7 _____   8 _____   9 _____   10 _____

4 In this set of exercises, modulations will be to the sub-dominant (IV), dominant (V) or the relative minor (R). Write down where the music modulates to and the name of the new key.

1 _____   2 _____

3 _____   4 _____

5 _____   6 _____

Section 5

Listening to music

In addition to discussing musical features, in Grade 7 you will be asked to suggest a possible composer. This doesn't mean you'll need to know *precisely* who wrote the piece, but to pick a name from the right historical period. Here are some well-known composers from each period. If you know any more, add them to the lists.

Baroque	**Classical**	**Romantic**	**20th/21st century**
Bach	W. A. Mozart	Schumann	Bartók
Handel	Haydn	Chopin	Stravinsky
Vivaldi	Clementi	Liszt	Copland
Purcell	Turk	Tchaikovsky	Shostakovich
Scarlatti		Brahms	Malcolm Arnold
		Albeniz	John Williams
		Grieg	

You may notice that a number of famous names do not feature in the list (Beethoven, Debussy and Rachmaninov, for example). These composers are harder to classify as their compositional style puts them in more than one period. It's sometimes misleading to think of composers fitting into neat categories.

 CD1 track 20

1 Listen to the examples on this track and connect the boxes. Think carefully about the features that lead you to your answers.

Bach	played 1st
W. A. Mozart	played 2nd
Tchaikovsky	played 3rd
Malcolm Arnold	played 4th

2 Suggest a composer for each of these pieces.

1 _____   2 _____

3 _____   4 _____

5 _____   6 _____

3 Look at the pieces you are currently learning and make a list of the important features that help you to identify the period. Beware of red herrings!

> You can practise working at this question whenever you hear some music. As you're listening, think about the following:
>
> - What did you notice about the dynamic levels?
> - Where there any tempo changes?
> - Do passages or sections return?
> - Was it major or minor? Did it modulate to new keys?
> - What textures did you notice?
> - Are there any interesting rhythmic features?
> - How would you describe the articulation?
> - How would you describe the character and style of the music?
> - What period does it come from?
> - Who might have composed the piece?

4 The pieces on the next six tracks explore all the features you might be asked about. Each will only be played once and then you'll be asked two questions. Complete each question by suggesting a possible composer.

1 _____

_____

2 _____

_____

Composer _____

1 _____

_____

2 _____

_____

Composer _____

CD1 track 24

1 _____

_____

2 _____

_____

Composer _____

CD1 track 25

1 _____

_____

2 _____

_____

Composer _____

CD1 track 26

1 _____

_____

2 _____

_____

Composer _____

CD1 track 27

1 _____

_____

2 _____

_____

Composer _____

5 Using a piece you are currently working on, answer the following:

• How would you best describe the character of the music? Why?

_____

• In which period was the piece written? Write down two reasons for your answer.

_____

_____

• Is the piece in a major or minor key?

_____

Rhythm

Listening activities

 1 In these exercises respond to each phrase with your own improvised rhythmic answer. Try to incorporate patterns you hear in your answer. You could clap or tap your answer or use two drumsticks or even spoons. Improvise! Each phrase is four bars in length.

Now repeat this track and simply clap back what you hear.

 2 Another improvisation, but this time make each 'answer' a real contrast with the 'question'. Now repeat this track and simply clap back the rhythms of each phrase.

 3 Now clap back the rhythm of each phrase as accurately as you can – each will only be played once. Don't worry if you're not absolutely precise. Be confident!

 4 The next set of examples will be played twice. Write down, as best you can, what you hear.

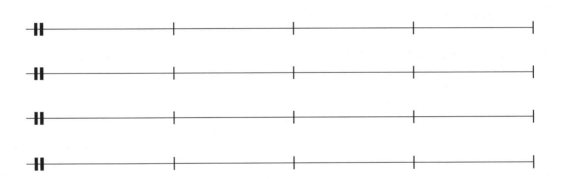

 5 In these examples, clap back each rhythm after you've heard it twice, as in the exam. Then write down the time signature. Listen carefully for the upbeat in numbers 2, 8 and 9.

1 ____   2 ____   3 ____   4 ____   5 ____

6 ____   7 ____   8 ____   9 ____   10 ____

6 Using a piece you are currently learning, clap or tap the rhythm of the whole piece with your right hand (on a table for example) and the pulse with your left hand. Now repeat swapping hands. Now tap the pulse with your right foot and clap or tap the rhythm.

Now try to hear the first four bars in your head, and then, without the looking at the music, have a go at answering the following questions:

1 What is the time signature? _____

2 Does the piece have an upbeat? _____

3 Is it in simple or compound time? _____

4 Are there any rests in the first four bars? _____

5 Write down the rhythm of the melody of the first four bars. Put in the time signature:

Come back and repeat this exercise using other pieces or using other four-bar phrases from the same piece.

Section 7

Making connections

Here are some musical activities that show you how aural connects with all the other areas of music. Choose one or two each time you practise.

... with theory

Each degree of the scale has a technical name – you've already met *tonic*, *sub-dominant* and *dominant*. Here are the rest:

Tonic	comes from the word *tone* (from the Latin *tonus* meaning 'sound')
Supertonic	above the tonic (from the Latin meaning 'above')
Mediant	mid-way between the tonic and dominant (from the Latin 'to be in the middle')
Sub-dominant	below the dominant (from the Latin 'below')
Dominant	after the tonic, the next most important chord in a key
Sub-mediant	mid-way between the sub-dominant and top tonic
Leading note	so called because of its pull towards the tonic
Tonic	

Listen to each of these phrases and decide on which degree of the scale they end. Use their technical names.

1 _____ 2 _____ 3 _____

4 _____ 5 _____ 6 _____

7 _____ 8 _____

... with inversions

Most chords can exist in three different positions: Root position, 1st and 2nd inversions. Here is a C major chord written in each 'position':

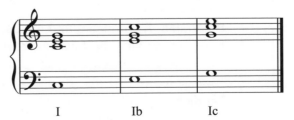

I   Ib   Ic

On this track you will hear either root position chords (R) or first inversion (1). Write down the correct position:

1 ____ 2 ____ 3 ____ 4 ____ 5 ____

6 ____ 7 ____ 8 ____ 9 ____ 10 ____

CD2 track 4

On this track the chords will be either root position (R) or second inversion (2). Write down the correct position:

1 _____   2 _____   3 _____   4 _____   5 _____

6 _____   7 _____   8 _____   9 _____   10 _____

...with sight-reading

Choose a sight-reading piece (from *Improve your sight-reading! Grade 7* for example) and try to hear the piece in your head. Then play it.

...with intervals

Play a note and then, in your head, hear the note a major 7th above (e.g. play C and then hear B). Sing the note and then play it to see how accurate you were. Can you find any major 7ths in the pieces you are currently studying?

...with dance styles

CD2 track 5

Using the information given in the boxes, work out the order the examples are played on the track, and write the number in the box.

> **Sarabande** Usually slow and steady. Three beats in a bar with a slight emphasis on the second beat.

> **Gavotte** A dance in moderate tempo usually beginning on the half bar.

> **Mazurka** Polish folk dance in triple time with a lively tempo, often with dotted notes as a feature.

> **Waltz** An elegant, charming dance in triple time.

> **Polonaise** A grandiose and majestic dance in triple time, often using the following rhythm: ¾ ♪♪♪♪♪♪♪ |

> **Ländler** A simple, robust folk dance in triple time, the precursor of the waltz.

> **Bourrée** Usually a light, lively dance in duple time.

The answers to all the questions in this book are available to download in PDF format from fabermusic.com

Grade 8

Pitch

Singing (or playing) the lowest part of a three-part phrase

If you've worked through the Grade 7 material you will have already met singing the lowest of three parts. (If you haven't, go back to Grade 7, Section 1, Exercise 5 on page 4.) It's really no more demanding than singing the lower of two parts, but you do need to concentrate your listening carefully. All examples in Grade 8 are four bars long.

Listening activities

1 On this track you'll hear some typical phrases played first without the upper two parts. They are really quite straightforward! Sing each example after you've heard it just once. Then you'll hear the same phrase again with the upper parts added. Again sing back the tune in the lowest part.

2 It is important to feel the pulse when singing back the lowest part. In this set of examples feel the pulse strongly and write down in which bar (1, 2, 3 or 4) the long note appears.

1 __2__   2 __4__   3 _____   4 __4__

NB Example 3 begins on an upbeat so listen particularly carefully.

3 Because the Grade 8 melodies are the lowest of *three* parts, they will probably be fairly low in pitch, so soprano and alto voices will need to find a comfortable octave at which to sing them. If you've worked through previous *Improve your aural!* books, you will already have practised this. On this track you'll hear some low melodies. Sing them back at your own comfortable octave. Each one will be played only once.

4 Listen carefully to each of these examples (played twice) and then sing the lowest part. It will then be repeated for you to check your answer. Simply stay cool, calm and collected and concentrate carefully.

Cadences

After you've sung back the lowest part you'll hear a continuation of the phrase and will then be asked to identify the cadence at the end. It will be either perfect, imperfect, interrupted or, new for the grade, *plagal*. (The word comes from the Greek meaning 'sideways'.) The plagal cadence is sometimes known as the 'amen' or the 'church' cadence.

The plagal cadence is formed by the chords IV – I.

IV   I

You'll hear some examples on CD2 track 11.

5 On this track you'll hear each of the four cadences played in a particular style. Connect the boxes.

Baroque		Perfect cadence
Classical		Plagal cadence
Romantic		Imperfect cadence
20th/21st century		Interrupted cadence

6 Now listen to each of these short phrases which end with either a perfect (P), imperfect (I), plagal (Pl) or interrupted (In) cadence. Write down the cadence.

1 _____   2 _____   3 _____   4 _____   5 _____   6 _____

Identifying chords

This is often found to be a challenging part of the aural tests because there are so many possibilities. But if you approach this musically it does become easier and more logical.

You can identify chords either by their technical names (tonic, dominant, seventh etc.) or by roman numerals (I, V^7 etc.). We suggest using the numerals as it will help you to know exactly where you are, relative to the keynote.

7 Listen to and memorise this famous theme from Minuet in G (from the Anna Magdelena Notebook). It contains at least one example of every note in the scale. Now hear the tune in your head, stopping at random notes, then identify which degree of the scale that particular note is. Repeat this exercise a number of times.

8 Listen to the following groups of four chords, paying particular attention to the bass line. Write down the degree of the scale for every bass note (they all start on the first degree or keynote).

1 _____   2 _____   3 _____

9 In each of these exercises you will hear four chords. Write down the cadence formed by the last two.

1 _____   2 _____   3 _____   4 _____

10 Listen to the track again and this time write down the chord names that constitute the cadence.

1 _____   2 _____   3 _____   4 _____

Chords

Here is a list of the chords you'll need to know and whether they are major or minor. Learn this list.

In a major key

Chord I (and its inversions)	MAJOR
Chord II (and its inversions)	MINOR
Chord IV	MAJOR
Chord V and V^7	MAJOR
Chord VI	MINOR

In a minor key

Chord I (and its inversions)   MINOR

(Chord II is a diminished chord and is unlikely to be used)

Chord IV	MINOR (in rare occasions this could be major)
Chord V and V^7	MAJOR (in rare occasions this could be minor)
Chord VI	MAJOR

11 Listen to the four chords in each of the following examples paying particular attention to the bass line. Only root position chords will be used. Write down the two final chords in each case. The first is done for you.

1 _II V^7_____   2 _____   3 _____

4 _____   5 _____   6 _____

Chord progressions

These are a little like familiar spoken expressions such as 'How are you?', 'Do you have a good reed?', or 'I play the piano, do you play too?'

The chord progressions that you will have to identify always end with a cadence – that takes care of the final two chords. Then there will be one or two 'lead-in' chords.

Here are some common examples. Listen to this track to hear them.
(Do this often – each has a particular sound that will soon become familiar.)

Leading to a perfect cadence

Ib V I

IIb V^7 I

IV I V I

IV Ic V I

II Ic V I

Leading to a plagal cadence

V IV I

VI IV I

IIb I IV I

Vb I IV I

Leading to an imperfect cadence

Ib I V

Ib IV V

VI IV V

Leading to an interrupted cadence

IIb V^7 VI

Ib IV V^7 VI

Ic V VI

12 Here are some chord progressions for you to identify. The first one is done for you.

1 $\underline{V\ IIb\ V^7\ I}$ 2 _____   3 _____

4 _____   5 _____   6 _____

7 _____   8 _____   9 _____

10 _____

Sight-singing from notation

In Grade 8 you will have to sight-sing the lower of two parts.

Listening activities

 1 Hear each of the following phrases in your head. Look carefully for scale and arpeggio patterns and how the music relates to the keynote. Then listen to the track. Each will have two melodic changes. Circle the notes that have been altered.

 2 Now sing each phrase as it is written; the track will give you the key chord for each example. After a pause you will hear the phrase played.

3 All the following examples have an upper part added. Study each example, hearing it as best you can in your head first. Look out for scale and arpeggio patterns and see how the two lines relate to each other. Then play the track and sing the lower part, pausing between each example.

Modulations

In Grade 8 the number of possible modulations is extended to eight keys – four major keys and four minor keys. Here is the list that you need to learn:

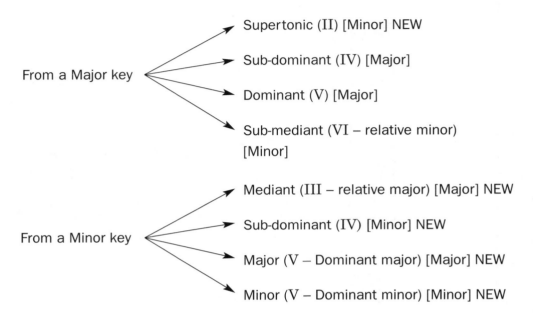

From a Major key
- Supertonic (II) [Minor] NEW
- Sub-dominant (IV) [Major]
- Dominant (V) [Major]
- Sub-mediant (VI – relative minor) [Minor]

From a Minor key
- Mediant (III – relative major) [Major] NEW
- Sub-dominant (IV) [Minor] NEW
- Major (V – Dominant major) [Major] NEW
- Minor (V – Dominant minor) [Minor] NEW

 CD2 track 23

Listen to this track (and repeat it often to get used to the sound of each modulation).

You will notice that each of the four destination keys have two major and two minor possibilities. So, if you know your keys, looking on the bright side, you'll always have a 50/50 chance of getting the answer right!

Listening activities

 CD2 track 24

1 In each of this set of examples just write down whether the destination key is major (M) or minor (m).

1 _____   2 _____   3 _____   4 _____

5 _____   6 _____   7 _____   8 _____

CD2 track 24

2 Now listen to track 24 again and write down exactly which key the music has modulated to and its relationship to the starting key.

1 _____   2 _____   3 _____   4 _____

5 _____   6 _____   7 _____   8 _____

Listening to music

In Grade 8 you will be invited to talk about a short piece played by the examiner. No specific questions will be asked at first. You will also be expected to suggest a composer. Have a look at the list of composers given in Grade 7, Section 5 (page 12) and add a few more names to each period through your own research. Also add a pre-baroque section.

The main areas for discussion will be melody and rhythm, tonality and harmony, articulation and dynamics, form, texture and character.

Ultimately it is the combination of a number of these features that will add up to the identification of the style and period. Listen intelligently to as much music as you can. You will soon begin to make a good attempt at identifying the style.

1 Listen to the simple melody on track 25. It could have been written any time between 1600 and 2008! Then you'll hear it dressed up in all sorts of musical 'costumes' that will point to a particular period. Connect the correct boxes:

Pre-baroque	played 1st
Baroque	played 2nd
Classical	played 3rd
Romantic	played 4th
20th/21st century	played 5th

2 Now suggest a composer for each of the pieces. You may want to listen to the track again.

Piece 1 _____   Piece 2 _____

Piece 3 _____   Piece 4 _____

Piece 5 _____

3 Look at the pieces you are currently learning and make a list of the important features that help to identify the period. Beware of red herrings!

4 This is for the really keen (but do have a go – it really will help you!). On a piece of paper write a short paragraph describing the main features of each style.

Rhythm	Syncopation Regular/Irregular Dotted Dance-like Simple/Complex
Melody	Scalic/Arpeggiated Cantabile Chromatic/Diatonic Beautiful/Ugly
Tonality	Diatonic Atonal Whole tone Modal
Dynamics	Constant Extreme Crescendo/Diminuendo etc.
Articulation	Legato Staccato Accents
Harmony	Diatonic Chromatic Complex/Simple Dissonant
Texture	Monophonic Tune with accompaniment Contrapuntal Chordal
Form	Binary Ternary Repetition Variation

Here's a useful list of words that you might like to learn and draw upon when describing music:

5 The pieces on the next five tracks combine all the features you might be asked about. Each will only be played once, then write a short paragraph about the music, mentioning as many significant features as you can. Complete each by suggesting a composer.

CD2 track 26

1 _____

_____

_____

Composer _____

CD2 track 27

2 _____

_____

_____

Composer _____

CD2 track 28

3 _____

_____

_____

Composer _____

CD2 track (29) **4** _____

_____

_____

Composer _____

CD2 track (30) **5** _____

_____

_____

Composer _____

6 Using a piece you are currently working on, answer the following:

• How would you best describe the character of the music? Why?

_____

• In which period was the piece written? Write down the reasons for your answer.

_____

_____

• Is the piece in a major or minor key? Does it modulate? Where to?

_____

Making connections

Here are some musical activities that show you how aural connects with all the other areas of music. Choose one or two each time you practice.

... with theory

Find a hymn book and, choosing a few bars, analyse the chords using roman numerals. Here is an example:

Now try to hear the chords in your head. Finally play them (or get a friend to play them) on the piano.

...with sight-reading

Choose a sight-reading piece (from *Improve your sight-reading! Grade 8* for example) and try to hear the piece in your head. Then play it.

...with intervals

Play a note and then, in your head, hear the note a Minor 7th above (e.g. play C and then hear B flat). Sing the note and then play it to see how accurate you were. Can you find any Minor 7ths in the pieces you are currently studying?

...with pastiche

Twentieth- and twenty-first-century composers often use styles from the past and dress them in contemporary clothes. Stravinsky, for example, often borrowed features from the baroque style – this kind of writing is termed *neo-baroque*, *neo-classical* or *neo-romantic*.

Listen to the pieces on CD2 track 31 and connect the boxes.

Neo-baroque	played 1st
Neo-classical	played 2nd
Neo-romantic	played 3rd

...with developing your critical faculty

 On this track you'll hear three performances of a Bach Minuet. Listen to them carefully. Now take on the role of a radio broadcaster writing for a review programme that compares and discusses different performances and then recommends the best for the public to go out and buy.

_____

_____

_____

_____

_____

_____

_____

_____

_____

_____

_____

_____

_____

_____

_____

fabermusic.com

© 2009 by Faber Music Ltd
First published in 2009 by Faber Music Ltd
74–77 Great Russell Street, London WC1B 3DA
Design by Susan Clarke
Printed in England by Caligraving Ltd
All rights reserved

ISBN10: 0-571-53281-0
EAN13: 978-0-571-53281-0

The text paper used in this publication is a virgin fibre product that is manufactured in the UK to ISO 14001 standards. The wood fibre used is only sourced from managed forests using sustainable forestry principles. This paper is 100% recyclable.

Grade 7 CD created by Ned Bennett and John Lenehan
Grade 8 CD created by Ned Bennett
Thanks to Godstowe School Chamber Choir 2006
CD1 track 20 and CD2 track 31 ℗ and © 1988-2009, licensed by kind permission of Naxos Rights International Ltd
All other tracks
℗ 2009 by Faber Music Ltd
© 2009 by Faber Music Ltd

To buy Faber Music publications or to find out about the full range of titles available please contact your local retailer or Faber Music sales enquiries:

Faber Music Limited, Burnt Mill, Elizabeth Way, Harlow CM20 2HX England
Tel: +44 (0) 1279 82 89 82   Fax: +44 (0) 1279 82 89 83
sales@fabermusic.com   fabermusic.com